MANDALAS
For Fun and Relaxation 2

ADULT COLORING BOOK

Vanessa Bentley

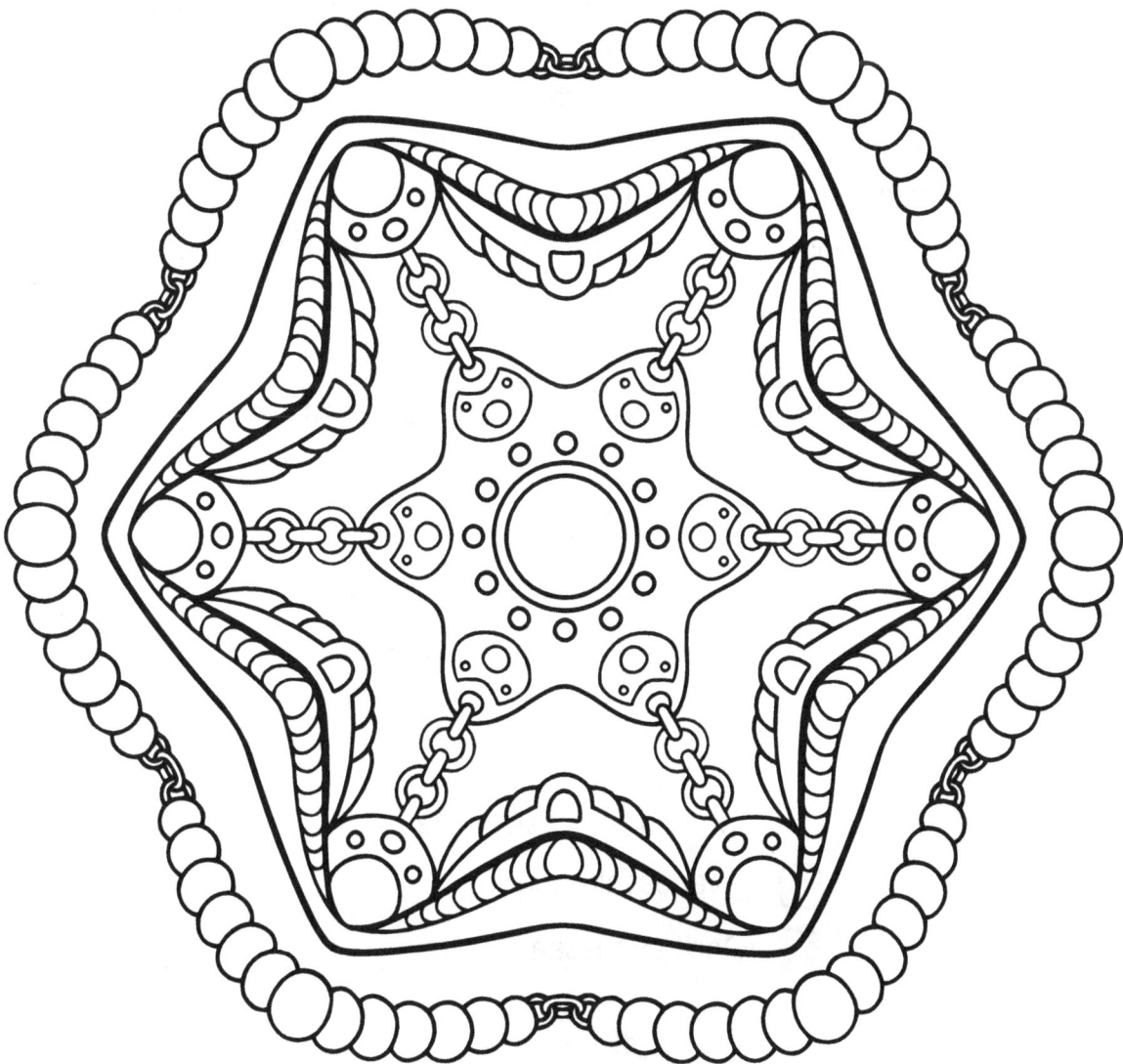

www.vanessabentley.com

Published in 2018 by

Stubby Pencil Press

Copyright © Vanessa Bentley 2018

ISBN-13: 978-0-620-79064-2
ISBN-10: 0620790644

50 Original Mandalas for you to color. Some are really easy and some are complex enough to keep your mind off all your worries for a few hours.

A variety of materials can be used to color these images, from color pencils to markers. To prevent bleed-through when coloring, place a blank sheet of paper between the pages.

Images have been printed on one side of the page only.

All images in this book are original drawings and designs by Vanessa Bentley.

Visit www.vanessabentley.com

Sign up for my newsletter

Subscribers get:

- Free coloring pages to download
- News of upcoming releases
- Giveaways and contests

You can also follow me on

[Instagram] @vanessabentleyart

[Facebook] @artbyvanessa

STUBBY PENCIL PRESS

I have always found drawing to be a great way to relax and unwind. When I'm stressed or just need to take my mind off my work, I'll grab one of my sketchbooks and draw or doodle. This is when I get lost for hours on end creating drawing after drawing, and I usually color them in with pens, markers and even highlighters.

The process of drawing and coloring in is so peaceful, it quiets the mind and helps me to let go of all my worries. All the stress of the day melts away with every stroke of the pen and my mood lifts with every bright color I use.

The simplicity or complexity of my drawings depends on my mood at the time. I hope that you will enjoy coloring them as much as I enjoyed drawing them.

There are no rules to coloring these designs, just enjoy them and have fun.

Vanessa Bentley

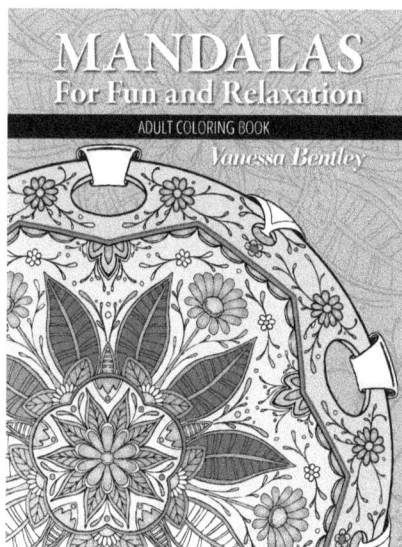

Also by Vanessa Bentley

MANDALAS For Fun and Relaxation

Mandalas

"Mandala" is a Sanskrit word that means "circle"

Mandalas have been around for centuries and it has been discovered that drawing or coloring mandalas is relaxing and uplifting. Mandala patterns are repeated around a centre point. Some designs are basic and simple while others can be very detailed and complex.

Although Mandalas mostly consist of abstract shapes, modern Mandalas can consist of animals, flowers and even figures or faces.

Some Mandalas in this book are very simple. You can color them as they are, but if you are feeling adventurous you can always take a pen and add your own touches to the mandala.

The Benefits of Coloring

Not everyone can draw or paint, that is where coloring books are great. The artist creates the image and puts it out there for someone else to complete the work by adding color in the medium of their choice. Many coloring book artists are pleasantly surprised when they get to see how colorists bring their images to life. So the artist and colorist are now in fact collaborators in the project.

Participating in a creativity such as coloring in occupies the part of the brain that deals with stress and worry. How? Well, when you color in you have to decide what you are going to color, what medium to use, what color or color combinations you are going to use and how you are going to color it.

Many retirement homes have started giving coloring pages to their residents to color in. It is not only good for hand eye coordination, but it is uplifting, relaxing and gives people a sense of accomplishment.

How to Color in

I believe that you should go with what you feel. Practice makes perfect and as you color more and more, you will get to know which colors you like putting together. If you are worried that you will mess up your image, you may make a copy of the page and practice on that copy.

Use the page provided to test your art materials and color combinations

If you want to learn more about coloring techniques, there are many tutorials on YouTube that will help you advance as a colorist.

Happy coloring!

You can use this page to test your art materials

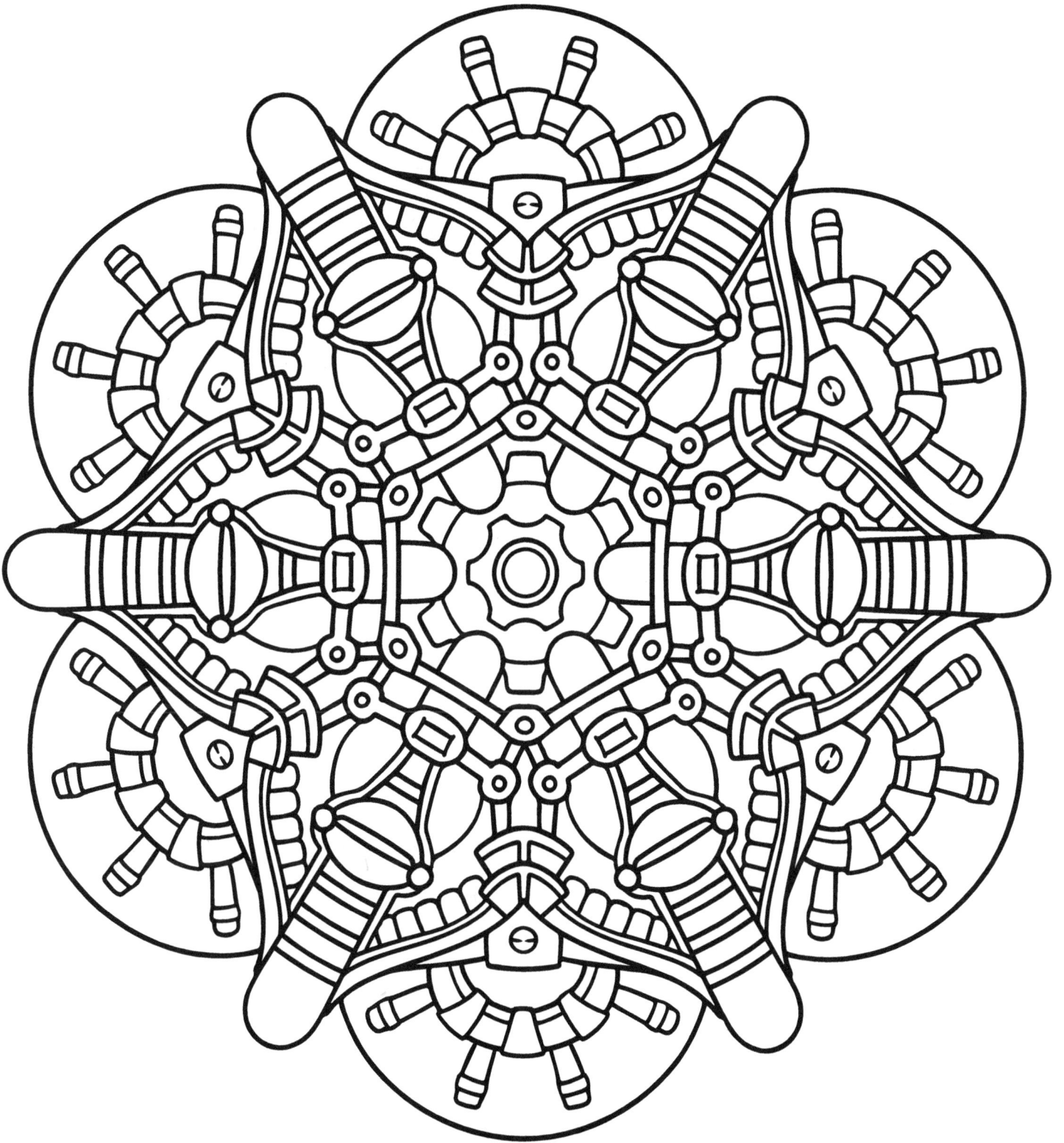

www.ingramcontent.com/pod-product-compliance
Lightning Source LLC
Chambersburg PA
CBHW081658270326
41933CB00017B/3215